T0380341

# Special Childhood Treasures

Verlinda J. Allen

Order this book online at www.trafford.com
or email orders@trafford.com

Most Trafford titles are also available at major online book retailers.

**www.trafford.com**
**North America & international**
toll-free: 844 688 6899 (USA & Canada)
fax: 812 355 4082

**Verlinda J. Allen**
**Bookspublished1@gmail.com**



ISBN: 978-1-6987-1004-4 (sc)

ISBN: 978-1-6987-1007-5 (e)

Print information available on the last page.

Trafford rev. 01/31/2022

# Table of Contents

**Published by The Library of Poetry*
***Published Elsewhere*

# Dedication

*These collection of poems, Special Childhood Treasures, are dedicated to My Miracle Baby, Zacharrias Daniel Hosein. The day you were born was truly a miracle of life.*

*To Shams, thank you for your input and ideas with Marbles and Sticks.*

*I love you, both, now and forever ... the journey has just begun.*

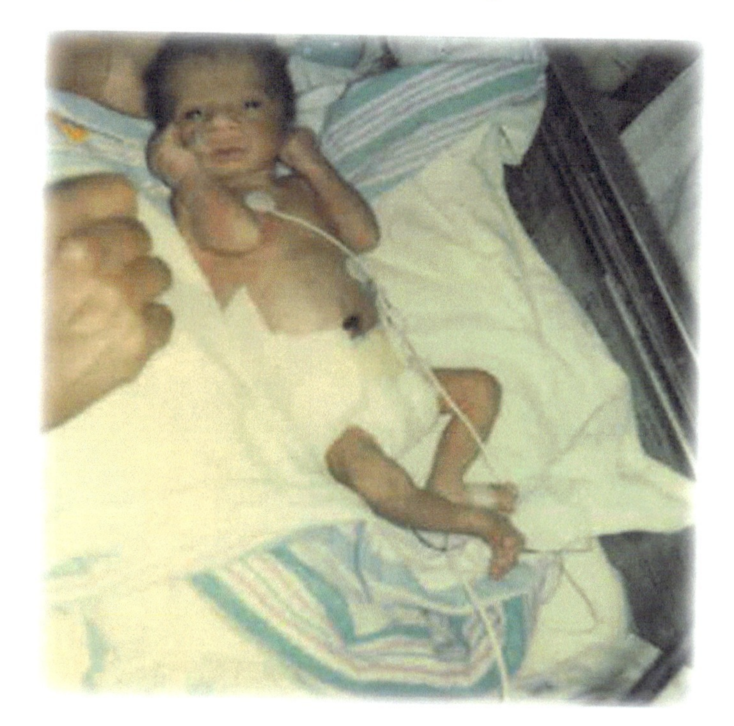

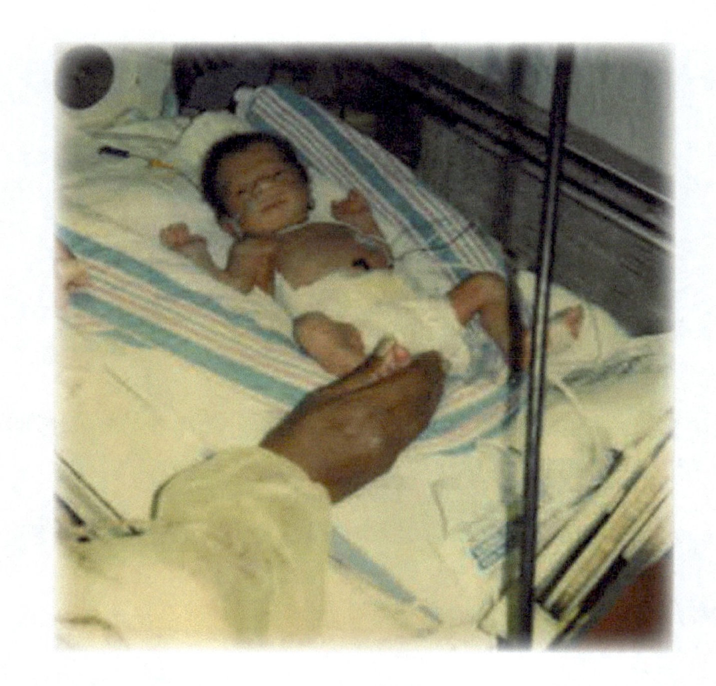

Zacharrias Daniel
Hosein
Born 7/19/06
3lbs, 14 1/2
18ins long

# *Kaleidoscope*

***Yellow, Red, Black and Blue***
***Oh, what wonderful colors you will see!***
***There's Purple, Pink, White and Orange too,***
***Locked within my kaleidoscope.***

***It's oh so magical to see***
***The colors that keep changing before me!***
***First, to Green,***
***Now, back to Yellow***
***The colors of my kaleidoscope you see.***

# *White*

***A colorless page,***
***A blinding light,***
***Clouds that float in the sky.***

***A fluffy kitten,***
***Or, soft woolen mittens;***
***That keep your hands toasty and warm ...***

***Oh, I hope never to be that color;***
***For it would be so hard to stay clean***
***Since I love to play in the dirt.***

# Purple

*What is the color of violets?*
*What is the color of amethysts?*
*What is red and blue combined?*

*It's my favorite color;*
*The color purple!*
*And it's oh so very fine.*

# *The Color Of The Rainbow*

***It comes in many colors,***
***The color of the RAINBOW,***
***It holds the brilliance of the sun.***

***You can see the colors very clearly,***
***After a heavy rainstorm …***
***BIG,***
***BRIGHT,***
***And BEAUTIFUL,***
***In the sky above;***
***Or reflected in a pool of water,***
***On the ground below.***

***The color of the RAINBOW***
***Is really a joy to see.***
***One of God's never ending Promises,***
***The magnificent RAINBOW***
***You see.***

# The World Is A Rainbow (Fri., 7/20/12)

*They say the world is a rainbow*
*With all the different people you see.*
*They come from all around the world,*
*Meeting in one big melting pot.*

*They say the world is a rainbow*
*So many languages that we speak,*
*And so many cultures to celebrate*
*Giving us a glimpse into our vast education.*

*They say the world is a rainbow*
*So many different barriers to over come.*
*One day, we can get past them;*
*To truly live as one.*

# The Solar System

*The Solar System,*
*Has nine planets in all:*
*Mercury, Venus, Earth, Mars, Jupiter, Saturn,*
*Uranus, Neptune and Pluto.*
*Each one in its own orbit,*
*Revolves around the sun.*
*One even has an outer ring.*
*Do you know which planet it is?*

*The Solar System,*
*With its different sized planets;*
*Ranging from big to small ...*
*And even in between.*
*The biggest is Jupiter,*
*While the smallest is Pluto,*
*The ninth and last planet.*
*It resembles a tiny dot among the stars.*
*Studies show that its not really a planet*
*But a ball of ice in space.*

*The Solar System,*
*Is a heavenly sight*
*As well as a scientist's absolute delight!*
*Discovering what is out there,*
*Teaching us the many different wonders*
*Of our universe.*

# Dream Maker, Star Maker

*Dream Maker, Star Maker*
*My ever true wish maker.*
*You see my dreams*
*My heartaches,*
*And pains,*
*My deepest heartfelt delights.*

*You make my inner most fantasies come true.*
*You help me rest when nights are long,*
*And help me to dream of what I long to do;*
*You let me,*
*Be me.*

*Some things I dream may be silly,*
*Or maybe even fun;*
*Some things may even be considered dumb.*
*But all my dreams show how I feel-*
*Everything from wild to carefree.*

*Dream Maker, Star Maker*
*My ever true wish maker.*
*With you I will always have what I wished ...*
*In my dreams last night.*

# The Land Of Make Believe

*The land of make believe*
*Is a wonderous*
*Place to be.*
*Filled with imagination*
*Of things you want to do and see.*

*The land of make believe*
*Is where your dreams*
*Can come Alive!*
*Where your thoughts can guide you*
*To untold adventures, dangers and fun.*

*The land of make believe*
*Unlocks the child inside all of us ...*
*To create and to be,*
*Whatever we can possibly imagine.*

*The land of make believe*
*Can be beautiful as the story unfolds,*
*This I know firsthand ...*
*From the help from my imagination,*
*In my land of make believe.*

# Pegasus

*PEGASUS*
*My beautiful white-winged*
*Flying horse,*
*Your graceful wings expand*
*As you take off.*

*You reign Supreme*
*Among all the other horses,*
*You're the cherished pet*
*On Mount Olympus.*

*You have sweet patience*
*For those who are kind;*
*Like children,*
*The old,*
*And the blind.*
*A fairy tale that will last forever.*

*PEGASUS,*
*My beautiful white-winged*
*Flying horse,*
*You were meant for heights;*
*To soar,*
*And to Glide,*
*Among the BIG,*
*BLUE,*
*SKY.*

# *Ladybug*

***Ladybug or Lady Beetle,***
***Depending on how you feel.***
***It really doesn't matter what you're called;***
***You're still a pretty little creature to me.***

# *Caterpillar*

***Caterpillar, Caterpillar***
***Fuzzy little Caterpillar***
***You inch as you crawl,***
***As your head looks about***
***You create your little dance,***
***That no one else can do.***

***You're so very soft to the touch,***
***And ticklish on my flesh-***
***As you crawl up and down,***
***With no place in particular in mind.***
***You just go along your merry way.***

# Butterfly

*Butterfly, oh butterfly,*
*Pretty little butterfly.*
*Silently you flutter,*
*Landing here and there,*
*Never giving pause to think,*
*As to why you're really there.*

*You stop from flower to flower,*
*Like the tiny hummingbird.*
*But, of course, your wings are not as noisy,*
*When you hover there.*

*Your wings are brightly colored,*
*Or blank as a piece of paper*
*Your BIG,*
*Your Small,*
*But, very, very, beautiful.*

*Oh, what I wouldn't give,*
*To have your special grace;*
*To delight, to charm, to brighten a child's face.*
*One of God's smallest and delicate creatures,*
*The ever wonderin' butterfly.*

# *Fuzzie Wuzzie Was A Bear?*

***Some say Fuzzie Wuzzie was a bear!***
***And that Fuzzie Wuzzie had no hair!***
***How could that possibly be?!***
***A bear without any hair?***
***Is something that is most***
***UN-BEAR-ABLE***
***To See!***

# Creatures Of The Sea

*How many creatures of the sea can you see?*
*That live and swim among the water's deep,*
*Or play on the water's surface?*

*Some of them are Friendly,*
*And some are Not.*
*Some of them are very BIG,*
*And some are very Little.*
*Some of them are very Fat,*
*And some are just to Skinny.*
*But it really matters Not.*

*Oh, to be a Creature of the Sea,*
*Without a worry or care.*
*To swim and Play,*
*And Lie all Day,*
*On a Rock,*
*In the Warm Sunshine.*

# The Dancer

*As a bird flies high in the sky,*
*So does a dancer when he or she leaps …*
*As a bird glides gracefully in the sky,*
*So does a dancer when he or she leaps …*

*As a bird walks and struts with confidence down the street …*

*As the Dancer has the grace and poise*
*To stand with their head held high*
*To the sky …*

*So must I*
*Upon my two feet.*

# Dancer's Riddle

***Tiptoe, Tiptoe, Tiptoe,***
***Never letting my feet touch the floor.***
***On my toes I go;***
***Spinning, Spinning, Spinning,***
***Just like a top!***

***Long and graceful,***
***Tall and erect.***
***Up and Down, Up and Down,***
***On my toes I go,***
***Never wanting to stop!***

***Graceful as a swan!***
***Gliding across the floor.***
***Twirling Back and Forth;***
***Leaping high into the air.***

***Once the music stops,***
***The applauses will start.***
***As you take your bows.***

# *Snow*

***White and fluffy,***
***Soft and slushy.***
***Oh what a pretty sight to see.***
***From my window,***
***Inside where it's warm.***
***Where I'm safe of its sticking to me.***

# Rain

*A gentle drop,*
*Here and there.*
*Some more*
*Gentle drops*
*EVERYWHERE!*
*Oh no!*
*Look out!*
*For here it comes!*
*A great down pour from up above!*

# Sunshine (Sat., 8/4/12)

*Warm on my face*
*As I look to the sky.*
*Bright and blinding to my eyes*
*Making me smile as I close my eyes.*

*The sunshine follows me everywhere I go,*
*I can't seem to escape it.*
*When its really hot outside*
*I sweat so much.*

*Oh no, the sun is beginning to set outside*
*You know what that means?*
*No more sunshine anymore.*

# *Spring Is Finally Here!!*

***Once again Winter has fled,***
***Snow is gone and off the ground;***
***And the sun shines once more.***

***No more bulky clothes,***
***And no more colds,***
***Just looking forward to***
***Warm days,***
***And warmer nights;***
***As well as plenty of fun times ahead.***

# Summer

*Summer, Summer*
*Almost here*
*Time for fun;*
*And Summer sun.*
*Time to throw the books away,*
*For they will be there*
*Come this Winter.*

*Days to spend with your friends,*
*At the beaches,*
*Or somewhere like Great Adventure!*

*So sit back and relax,*
*And put on your head gear,*
*And wait for September to reappear.*

# Lazy Summer Day

*Oh what a lazy summer day.*
*Not much for me to do.*
*Inside is hot,*
*Outside even hotter.*

*Don't want to read,*
*Don't want to sleep,*
*Don't even want to eat.*

*All I want is some nice cool breeze*
*To come and put an end*
*To my consistent misery.*

*Oh what a lazy summer day.*
*Not much for me to do.*
*Just to sit outside and take a look around,*
*Before I finally jump in my neighbor's pool.*

# The Beach

*White sands,*
*Orange sands,*
*Depending where you go.*
*Calm seas*
*Of clear blue waters,*
*Or mucky greenish color.*

*Seashells by the dozen;*
*Varying from size to color.*
*Horseshoe crabs and land crabs;*
*The kind that hide in the sand.*

*People by the thousands,*
*Laying all about.*
*Trying to catch a bit of sunshine*
*While chillin' (coolin') by the sea.*

# *Vacation?-I*

***A vacation was all I ever wanted.***
***To slip away unnoticed***
***For a little bit of solitude.***

***But I never thought it would be***
***In a place with little activity!***
***Only sleep will do.***

***Or,***
***Sit and lie***
***Around my room***
***In the local hospital!***

# *Vacation?-II*

***Needles, I.V. fluids, tests …***
***Who needs it!***

***I do,***
***That's who.***

***My time to rest and get better.***
***Here once again***
***The story of my life***
***The hospital-***
***My second home for life.***

# *The Rose*

*The rose is a beautiful and delicate flower,*
*It comes in many shapes and colors;*
*From big to small,*
*To pink, white, red and yellow …*
*Even purple I'm told.*

*The rose is a special flower,*
*That is given to those we adore.*
*From friends to lovers,*
*And spouses to other family members and kin*
*It is sent with our deepest adoration and love.*

*The rose, a thing of beauty*
*With its delicate petals,*
*That lovingly open to show the beauty*
*That is held within.*

*Though dozens are given day-by-day,*
*To that special someone.*
*Even as it begins to wilt;*
*It's beauty never really dies.*

# The Color Of The Rose

*Each color of the rose,*
*Has a special meaning*
*That tells what each rose stands for ...*

*Pink, now represents friendship,*
*While Purple, is still for passion;*
*As everyone knows*
*Red, stands for love*
*And White, will continually be innocence, purity and truth.*

*The Black colored rose has always been death;*
*While the Yellow ...*
*How should we explain it ...*

*The Yellow rose has changed some-*
*It once represented friendship,*
*But now I'm told it has changed again;*
*This time to jealousy and unfaithfulness.*

*I've asked exactly what the Yellow stands for,*
*But, of course*
*No one is really sure.*

*But together,*
*Each rose represents*
*A display*
*Of a lovely bouquet.*

# *Marbles (Sat., 8/4/12)*

*Round and colorful,*
*Hard and cool.*
*An assortment of many different shapes.*

*I love to play with them,*
*As I watch their pretty colors.*
*I love to hold them close to my eyes*
*As I watch the light shine thru them.*

*I love to hold them between my fingers*
*Before I pitch them in the ring,*
*Watching as they hit against the others;*
*As they knock them out the ring.*

# *Sticks (Sat., 8/4/12)*

***Long or short***
***Fat or skinny,***
***I play with them as I walk with my parents.***

***Everywhere around me***
***I see them as they fall from the tree-***
***I love to bang them together or drum them against the tree.***

***Where did I drop it?***
***I know not where to find it;***
***Oh well, never mind***
***I see another stick right there.***

# *A Baby's First Laugh*

*The first time you hear it,*
*Its like music to your ears.*
*You tend to smile and often laugh too,*
*Hearing that infectious sound.*

*You can't help but continue*
*Just to hear that laugh-*
*Doing whatever it takes*
*To make the baby laugh.*

*That first initial baby's laugh*
*Is all that it takes-*
*You spend just about every waking hour*
*Hoping it persists.*

# My Baby Boy**

*(Appears in The Highs and Lows of Love; my 1st published book in print)*

*I watch you grow-*
*From 3, now 4*
*Your smile and curiosity growing everyday;*
*My little baby boy is coming into his own.*

*Who is this wonder I helped produce;*
*From that pale tiny creature that I had to wait to hold.*
*You're my baby boy who I love so much;*
*A little whirlwind of energy running pass my face.*
*You're like a hummingbird who goes from flower to flower;*
*Never getting tired.*

*To watch you sleep and touch your silky lashes;*
*You look so much like your Dad and I-*
*(even though he tells me I made a mini me)*
*You're so unique looking.*

*You have so many cultures that run thru your little veins;*
*Your Dad says you're of the new generation of kids,*
*(a multicultural race for the future).*
*That doesn't matter to me …*
*What matters is that you're my baby boy.*

# *My Miracle Baby***

***(Appears in The Highs and Lows of Love; my 1st published book in print)***

***The day you were born I couldn't even hold you;<br>You weren't breathing at first and had to be taken to the NICU (Newborn Intensive Care Unit).<br>The picture your father brought back of you was my proudest moment.<br>Yet, I couldn't believe how pale and small you were; three pounds fourteen and a half ounces!<br>I admit, I was afraid to finally hold you-<br>But, when I did I didn't want to let you go.<br>You felt so good and looked so peaceful sleeping in my arms.***

***Now, you have turned a year old;<br>Where your little smile continues to give me joy and missing satisfaction<br>That I lost as a kid.***

***You're my little miracle boy, Danny.<br>One day you will grow to be your own man.<br>Until that happens I'll steal every chance to hold you in my arms-***

***And cherish my moments with you.<br>Erasing all my sad and lonely times.<br>Thank you for changing my life;<br>My miracle child of mine.***

# The Laughter Of A Child*

***(Appears in The Library of Poetry Anthology … <u>Mirage</u>; 6th published poem in print)***

***The laughter of a child,***
***Is the sweetest sound to hear-***
***It's pure and innocent,***
***And filled with wonder.***

***The laughter of a child,***
***Can brighten a room***
***Or bring a smile***
***To an elderly person's face.***

***The laughter of a child,***
***Is untainted with worry,***
***Grief,***
***Or pain;***
***Nothing seems to daunt it.***
***It is of absolute freedom***
***When everything is filled with nothing but joy.***

***The laughter of a child,***
***Stays that way-***
***Until the child becomes an Adult.***
***Where Reality sets in;***
***Making the laughter … sometimes stops.***

# *If You Don't Have Your Dreams**

***(Appears in The Library of Poetry Anthology … A Painted Garden; 7th published poem in print)***

***If you don't have your Dreams***
***Then all you have is Nothing.***
***For your dreams are What,***
***Helps to keep you Alive.***

***Your dreams help you to See***
***What your future can be Like;***
***But it is up to You***
***To make it come to Light.***

***Your dreams are a part of what's You,***
***They help guide You***
***To what you feel is Right.***
***Your dreams come from your inner Light.***

***If you don't have your Dreams***
***Then all you have is Nothing.***
***You might as well sit and Wilt,***
***Like a flower does without its Water.***

# The Mirrors To One's Soul

*They say the eyes are the mirrors to one's soul.*
*That they can tell others of what you may feel.*

*A stranger who doesn't know you*
*Can easily learn about you;*
*Just by looking into your eyes.*
*Learning all about your secrets,*
*That which you want to hide.*

*It is not always easy*
*To hide what you feel,*
*Because your eyes will always show it;*
*While another's gaze is on you*
*And you won't even know it.*

*The mirrors to one's soul*
*Are our eyes you see,*
*They cannot hold the pain,*
*Or hurt inside.*
*They tell others what our words*
*Can't sometimes convey.*
*Never staying silent.*

*The mirrors to one's soul*
*Are the expression in our eyes …*
*Don't you see?*

# *Friendship*

*Friendship is a special gift*
*That is shared by so few,*
*Because no one is willing*
*To take the time*
*To trust in one another.*

*Nowadays,*
*No one is willing*
*To learn to share in the joy of being …*
*Helpful,*
*Without any demands.*

*That is what the world has come to;*
*Mistrust,*
*Jealousy,*
*And conceit.*
*Never really trusting*
*Because of hate and deceit …*

*How does one start a friendship?*
*By being just a friend.*
*One who is patient.*
*Understanding,*
*And willing to listen*
*To each other's point of views.*

*Doesn't anyone want a friendship?*
*I know I sure do …*
*So,*
*How about you?*

# My Best Friend

*My best friend*
*Is special to me,*
*Because of the caring bond*
*That we have shared.*

*It took patience, time and years,*
*For me to trust, understand and be carefree-*
*Not be the way I use to be;*
*Doubtful, fearful and meek.*

*Not many I can share my feelings with,*
*But with him it seems very simple ...*
*Not having to fear being Ridiculed,*
*Misjudged,*
*Or even falsely accused.*

*He isn't judgmental,*
*Or pushy.*
*Domineering ... Well?*
*He says he is.*
*Though I have yet to see it.*

*My best friend*
*Has been around for several years now.*
*We may not get to talk like we use to;*
*Yet, he is still there whenever I need him.*

# *My Special Talent*

*My writing is a special gift from God,*
*The words seem to flow:*
*From thought,*
*To pen,*
*And finally,*
*To the paper.*

*It was something that was undiscovered, until now.*

*Writing,*
*I'm told,*
*Takes a special talent.*
*Not many have it …*
*Capturing the reader's attention.*
*It takes time,*
*Patience,*
*And hard work!*
*As well as belief … in yourself!*

*My writing is how I express myself,*
*By putting my thoughts on paper;*
*From my joys,*
*To my pains.*
*It has blossomed*
*Into an extension of me.*

*Somethings can be shared*
*While others,*
*May not …*
*It could be to personal to talk about.*
*Yet,*
*It still has to come out!*

*Writing,*
*This dear and precious gift I have.*
*Can take me far,*
*Far,*
*Away,*
*When I'm deeply troubled;*
*Or want to just get away*
*I grab my pen and paper …*
*And dearest,*
*Friend.*

*This special gift from God above,*
*Is truly a Heavenly blessing,*
*Because it allows me*
*To share*
*My special talent*
*With you …*
*The reader.*

# Music

***Sounds of Melody,***
***Sounds of Harmony,***
***Vocal or Instrumental.***

***Lullabies or Hushabies,***
***Songs to make a Baby sleep.***

***It can make YOU SHOUT FOR JOY,***
***And make you STOMP YOUR FEET!***
***It can leave you wanting more.***

***Sometimes you will Cry,***
***Or maybe even Smile …***
***But ALWAYS it can leave a Tune within your head.***
***That makes you hum it Until time for bed.***

# *Songs On The Wind*

***I sometimes often Hear,***
***The Sounds Of Songs On The Wind,***
***Of Times Long Ago***
***Of Peaceful Harmony!***

***The Native American Indians***
***Who Sang And Chanted Around Their Tribal Fires,***
***Their Voices Would Carry***
***Like The Songs On the Wind.***
***Telling Of Their History:***
***Of Peace, Heartaches, Suffering, Blood Shed and Pain.***

***The Sounds Of Song On The Wind***
***Can Easily Be Heard***
***Out In The Open Country,***
***Where The City Traffic Noises***
***Cannot Bother It!***

# The African Drums

*Softly they thump*
*Setting a steady beat.*
*Giving those who hear it*
*Hope, comfort and peace.*

*Gentle as a lullaby*
*That of a mother's love to her child.*
*A gentle and loving embrace*
*That lovers share.*

*The African drums*
*Beats loud and strong.*
*Keeping alive our fore-fathers*
*Our familys' ancient history.*

*Life is a mystery*
*With many different wonders;*
*To see,*
*And to sometimes behold,*
*To dream of what's untold.*

*Life is a mystery*
*Dark,*
*As well as mysterious.*
*Often scary*
*And frightening to comprehend …*
*At times,*
*Its even hard to accept.*

*Life is a mystery*
*For you to embrace.*
*To take what is yours*
*And make it a part of your goal.*

# First Day Of School (Sun., 8/12/2012)

*The excitement of the day,*
*The frenzy of the weeks before*
*The first day of school*
*To never a dull moment.*

*Some children cry*
*While others smile and wave bye-bye*
*As parents watch proudly,*
*Their children go into school.*

*All the chaos*
*All the drama*
*No one knows how the day will be*
*But, I bet all are happy …*
*Once it ends.*

*The first day of school*
*Comes every year-*
*Come August or September*
*Every experience is a blessed one;*
*When your child retells his or her day.*

# *What Makes Halloween Fun*

***Candy, ghosts, goblins***
***Witches, costumes and fun***
***Are what makes Halloween special.***

***The ghostly stories,***
***The horror movies from Frankenstein to the Mummy.***
***The parties to midnight:***
***With dancing, pranks and apple bobbing.***

***Halloween trick-a-treaters***
***Race down the street***
***Going from house to house.***

***All of this is celebrated***
***On the night***
***Of October 31st!***

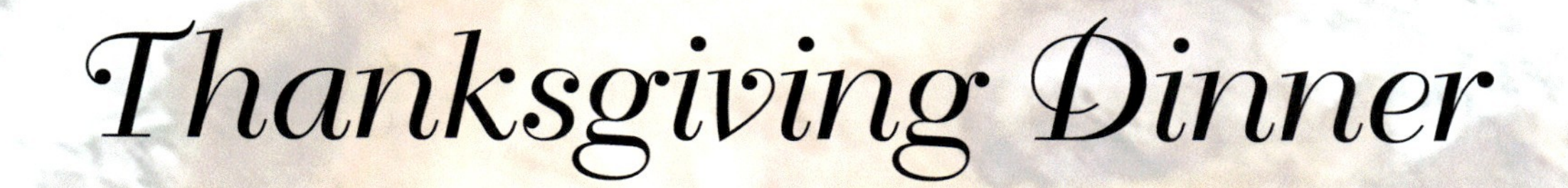


***Cranberry sauce, stuffing (yuck), turkey, string beans, collared greens, pumpkin pie and rice.***
***Gravy, mac and cheese, key lime pie, dutch apple pie and whipped topping.***
***Who can forget the egg nog …***
***What a beautiful dinner this will be!***

# Un-Bear-Able Christmas

***Christmas will be "un-bear-able" without you,***
***So don't be blue because we'll see one another***
***Once its through.***

# *Short Bunny Wish*

***Some Bunny is wishing you***
***A Hoppiest and joyous holiday.***
***Some Bunny is Hoppiest to say,***
***Merry Christmas to you-***
***And a very Bunny Hoppiest New Year!***

# *The Meaning Of Christmas*

***Though we celebrate the red and the green,***
***Santa Claus and presents;***
***Or family and friends-***
***Who gather among us,***
***This special time of the year.***
***Let us not forget***
***The true meaning of***
***This Blessed and Happy Day;***
***That the birth of Jesus Christ,***
***Was stated to be born this time of the year.***

# *Another Year*

***Well, another year has come to a close,***
***Time to reflect on the things that we have done.***
***Time for laughter;***
***Time to be merry.***
***It's just about time to welcome a brand New Year!***

# *We Sometimes Often Wonder**

***(Appears in Poetry Elite; 9th published poem in print)***

***We sometimes often wonder***
***Why we have so many heartaches,***
***But we never stop to wonder about others and their grief.***

***People who cannot help themselves,***
***Who are sometimes, helpless as babes.***
***Having to put their faith in others to be there for them.***

***Always we argue and always we complain …***
***Never once, giving thought to***
***Others and their pain.***

***The ones who are the less fortunate***
***Seem to have the biggest hearts.***
***While the so-called high and mighty,***
***Walk around with blinders … closing their eyes to***
***The pain-and often misery-surrounding them.***

***We all have to live here***
***On God's green earth;***
***We have to come together, to help one another,***
***To understand one another,***
***To stop killing each other … before it's too late.***

# *Imagine That*

***Imagine a world without any crime,***
***diseases, suffering, or pain.***
***Can you imagine that?***

***Imagine rainbow skies or sunny days,***
***warm weather and cooler nights.***
***Can you imagine that?***

***Is there such a perfect place?***
***Some say Heaven is such a place;***
***Peaceful, perfect and whole.***

***Can you truly imagine that.***

# *A Time To Remember**

***(Appears in The Library of Poetry Anthology … Songs on the Wind; 3rd published poem in print)***

***A time to remember,***
***To what we all shared?***
***We sometimes laughed,***
***And we sometimes cried.***
***We took the sweet times***
***Along with the bad.***

***There were special bonds formed,***
***With the friends we met along the way,***
***Who stood by you come what may.***

***But now that this special chapter,***
***Of our lives comes to a close;***
***We will each in our way***
***Look back on all the memories***
***That we have shared.***

***To smile,***
***To cry,***
***To laugh,***
***And sigh.***

***To look back on all our memories, and say, "What a time to remember."***

# Someone Asked Me A Question?(Yearbook)**

*(Part of The International Library of Poetry) (College Yearbook)*

*Someone asked me a question*
*Just thee other day.*
*As to what my plans would be*
*After Graduation Day.*

*I really couldn't say*
*Because I didn't have an answer.*
*The plain and simple truth was …*
*I just didn't know*
*One thing I can say, though.*
*It's not to Disney World.*

*Someone asked me a question*
*Just thee other day.*
*As to what my possible future would be,*
*After Graduation Day.*

*I guess I'll find a job in my degree*
*That's the most logical thing to me;*
*But first I'll go and celebrate*
*That's something I know I'll do;*
*On Graduation Day.*

# The Rising Phoenix**

*(Anaya Heart Infinity Slogan)*

*Out from the nighttime ashes*
*Arises the Phoenix,*
*Ever changing,*
*Ever growing;*
*Newly formed,*
*Until it rises on the next morn.*

*I am that Phoenix,*
*Changing at a whim.*
*Forming in new directions,*
*Taking on the world head on*
*Making a difference as I go-*
*Soaring and reaching new heights.*

# Missing You**

***(Appears in The Highs and Lows of Love; my 1st published book in print)***

*Here today and gone tomorrow*
*Thinking of you makes me sad and blue,*
*It only happens because I'm missing you.*
*Several miles separates the distance between us.*
*And then there may be no miles at all.*
*Still, there is nothing that I can do,*
*Because I only know*
*That I'm missing you.*

*You were a good friend,*
*Someone who was easy to talk to-*
*Sometimes, for long hours at a time.*
*Now that has changed,*
*Because you're nowhere in sight.*

*Don't know when we'll meet again,*
*Or, if you'll be back this way someday.*
*All I know is that our friendship*
*has been stretched,*
*To cover the distance where you're at.*

*Only time will tell if it will remain ever true,*
*Or, if it will die with the lonely years;*
*No longer hearing the sound of your voice,*
*Or smiling at the teasing manner you have.*

*All I can do is hope and pray,*
*To once again see you one day.*
*But until that time comes around,*
*I'll just keep on missing you.*

# My Grandma

*You were more to me*
*Then just my Grandma-*
*To me you were my mom.*
*You cared for me thru my illness;*
*Sitting for hours, rocking me.*
*You gave me the love I needed*
*That wasn't given by my mother.*

*Now, I feel the weight of your not being here-*
*I'm glad you lived long enough for my last visit and your final good-bye.*

*Seeing you that final summer was the end to my trips too;*
*I can't seem to bring myself to want to go with Danny-*
*Even though I miss Auntie as well.*

*I try to smile*
*Yet, its so damn hard …*
*The loss, pain and unbelievable hurt-*
*Missing you so much.*

*Tears start to flow*
*Thinking of the holidays and things I learned*
*From my Grandma,*
*My mother and friend.*

Printed in the United States
by Baker & Taylor Publisher Services